Velociraptor

Aaron Carr

AV2

Step 1
Go to **www.av2books.com**

Step 2
Enter this unique code

EBGNFUHLF

Step 3
Explore your interactive eBook!

AV2

MIGHTY DINOSAURS

Velociraptor

Start!

AV2 is optimized for use on any device

Your interactive eBook comes with...

Read
Audio
Listen to the entire book read aloud

Videos
Watch informative video clips

Weblinks
Gain additional information for research

Try This!
Complete activities and hands-on experiments

Key Words
Study vocabulary, and complete a matching word activity

Quizzes
Test your knowledge

Slideshows
View images and captions

View new titles and product videos at
www.av2books.com

MIGHTY DINOSAURS

Velociraptor

CONTENTS

Meet the Velociraptor.

Its name means "speedy thief."

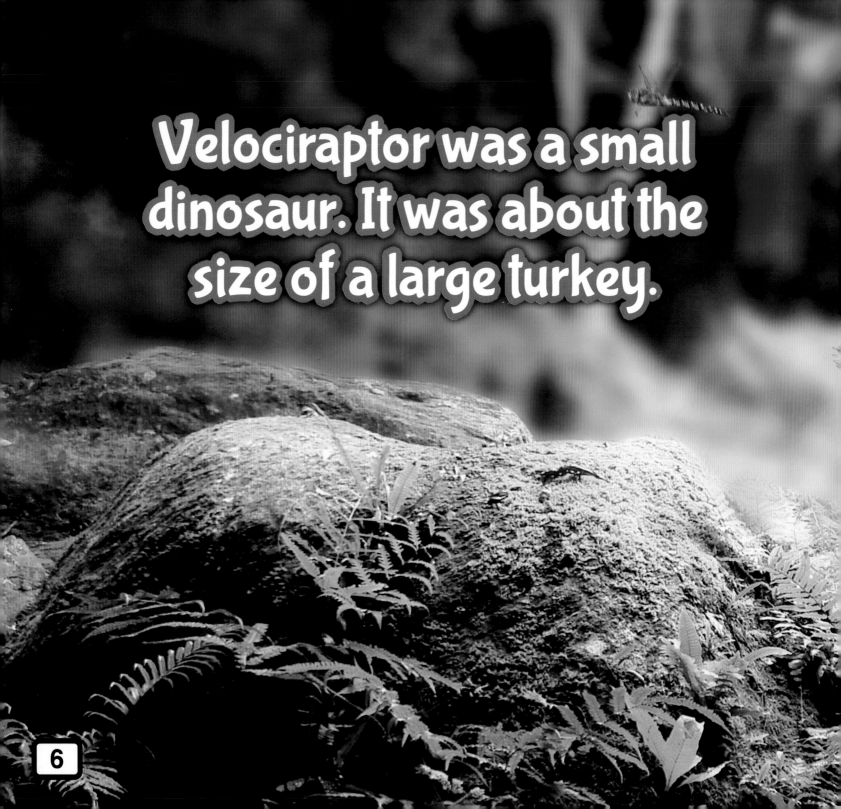

Velociraptor was a small dinosaur. It was about the size of a large turkey.

Velociraptor had a long, sharp claw on each foot.

It used these claws to catch its food.

Each Velociraptor claw was about 3.5 inches long.

9

Velociraptor was a meat eater. It hunted small plant-eating dinosaurs for food.

Velociraptor was one of the smartest dinosaurs that ever lived.

It may have hunted with other Velociraptors.

Velociraptor ran on two strong legs.

It may have run more than 40 miles an hour.

15

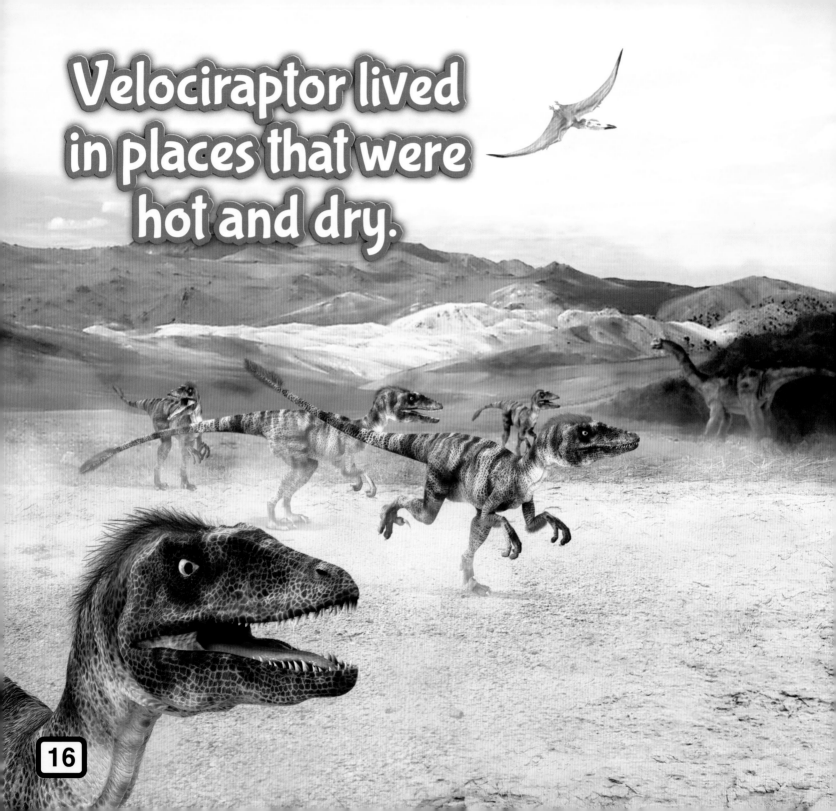

Velociraptor lived in places that were hot and dry.

It lived in parts of Asia.

Velociraptors died out about 80 million years ago.

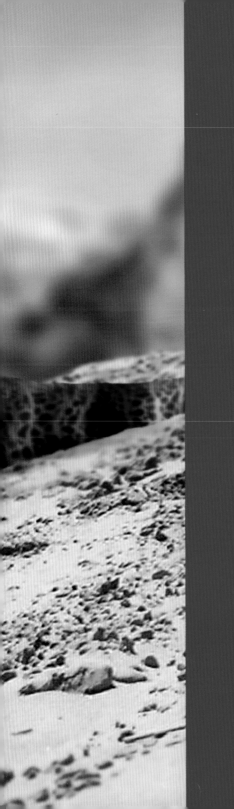

Velociraptor fossils formed over millions of years.

The American Museum
of Natural History in
New York displays
Velociraptor fossils.

People can go to museums to see fossils and learn more about the Velociraptor.

Velociraptor Facts

These pages provide detailed information that expands on the interesting facts found in the book. They are intended to be used by adults as a learning support to help young readers round out their knowledge of each amazing dinosaur or pterosaur featured in the *Mighty Dinosaurs* series.

Pages 4–5

Velociraptor means "speedy thief." The Velociraptor is one of the best-known of all dinosaurs. However, the real Velociraptor was very different from the one people know from movies such as *Jurassic Park*. Unlike the large, scaly raptors seen in movies, the real Velociraptor was much smaller and had feathers. Some scientists believe the Velociraptor may have been entirely covered in feathers, like a bird.

Pages 6–7

Velociraptor was a small dinosaur. The Velociraptor was about 6 feet (1.8 meters) long and 3 feet (1 m) tall. It may have weighed between 15 and 33 pounds (7 and 15 kilograms). Some relatives of the Velociraptor were larger than others. Deinonychus was the largest of these dinosaurs, with a length of 12 feet (3.7 m) and a weight of 150 pounds (68 kg). Most Velociraptors, however, were about the size of a large turkey.

Pages 8–9

Velociraptor had a long, sharp claw on each foot. Each sickle-shaped claw was 3.5 inches (9 centimeters) long. A retractable claw was located on the second toe of each foot. The Velociraptor used its claws to hunt for food and to defend itself from predators. Scientists believe the Velociraptor may have used its tail and one foot for balance while it slashed at its prey with the other foot.

Pages 10–11

Velociraptor was a carnivore, or meat-eater. Scientists believe the Velociraptor preyed on small herbivorous dinosaurs, such as Protoceratops and hadrosaurs. Many scientists believe the Velociraptor hunted in packs to take down larger prey. However, there is no direct evidence to support this theory. Some scientists have suggested that the Velociraptor may have been a scavenger.

Velociraptor was one of the smartest dinosaurs that ever lived. The Velociraptor was part of the dromaeosaur family of dinosaurs. These dinosaurs had large brains compared to other dinosaurs. Scientists estimate dinosaur intelligence by comparing the size of the dinosaur's brain to the overall size of its body. By this measure, dromaeosaurs such as the Velociraptor were second in dinosaur intelligence only to the Troodon.

Velociraptor may have been able to run more than 40 miles (60 kilometers) per hour. The Velociraptor was a bipedal, or two-legged, dinosaur. Its legs were long and thin. This, combined with the Velociraptor's light weight, made it one of the fastest of all dinosaurs. Scientists also think the Velociraptor could jump, which may have helped it catch food.

Velociraptor lived in hot, dry areas. The Velociraptor was native to Asia, with most species found in what is now the Gobi Desert area of Mongolia. In the Velociraptor's time, this part of the world had a desert climate. The climate was very similar to the climate this area has today, but warmer. The Velociraptor shared its habitat with other dinosaurs and several kinds of lizards.

Velociraptor lived about 80 million years ago during the Cretaceous Period. People know about the Velociraptor from fossils. Fossils are formed when an animal dies and is quickly covered in sand, mud, or water. This keeps the hard parts of the body, such as bones, teeth, and claws, from decomposing. The body is pressed between layers of mud and sand. Over millions of years, the layers turn into stone, and the dinosaur's bones and teeth turn into stone as well. This preserves the size and shape of the dinosaur.

People can go to museums to see fossils and learn more about the Velociraptor. Every year, people from around the world go to museums to see Velociraptor fossils. Many museums have permanent dinosaur fossil exhibits, while smaller museums tend to host traveling exhibits for short periods of time. The American Museum of Natural History in New York City has a permanent dinosaur display that features Velociraptor fossils, including a fossil showing a Velociraptor and a Protoceratops together.

KEY WORDS

Research has shown that as much as 65 percent of all written material published in English is made up of 300 words. These 300 words cannot be taught using pictures or learned by sounding them out. They must be recognized by sight. This book contains 48 common sight words to help young readers improve their reading fluency and comprehension. This book also teaches young readers several important content words, such as proper nouns. These words are paired with pictures to aid in learning and improve understanding.

Page	Sight Words First Appearance	Page	Content Words First Appearance
4	its, means, name, the	4	thief, Velociraptor
6	a, about, it, large, of, small, was	6	dinosaur, turkey
8	each, food, had, long, on, these, to, used	8	claw, foot, inches
11	for, plant	11	meat eater
12	have, lived, may, one, other, that, with	14	legs
14	two	15	hour
15	an, miles, more, run, than	17	Asia
16	and, in, places, were	19	fossils
17	parts	20	American Museum of Natural History, New York
18	out, years	21	museums
19	over		
20	American		
21	can, go, learn, people, see		

Published by AV2
350 5th Avenue, 59th Floor
New York, NY 10118
Website: www.av2books.com

Library of Congress Control Number: 2019950186

ISBN 978-1-7911-1672-9 (hardcover)
ISBN 978-1-7911-1673-6 (softcover)
ISBN 978-1-7911-1674-3 (multi-user eBook)

Printed in Guangzhou, China
1 2 3 4 5 6 7 8 9 0 24 23 22 21 20

022020
100919

Project Coordinator: Priyanka Das
Art Director: Terry Paulhus

Every reasonable effort has been made to trace ownership and to obtain permission to reprint copyright material. The publishers would be pleased to have any errors or omissions brought to their attention so that they may be corrected in subsequent printings.

All illustrations by Jon Hughes, pixel-shack.com. AV2 acknowledges Shutterstock and Wikimedia as its primary image suppliers for this title.